BROKEN DOLLS

Written by June Prager

Based on a Work by Melisa Tien

Published by

Blue Moon Plays

Your Once-in-a-Blue-Moon Experience

For production copies and information, please contact
Blue Moon Plays

Published by Blue Moon Plays
Blue Moon Plays, LLC
1385 Fordham Road, Ste 105-279
Virginia Beach, VA 23464
Editor: Maggie Douglas
Cover Photo Credit:

ISBN: 978-1-943416-78-3

BROKEN DOLLS

Broken Dolls by June Prager can be performed by community, educational, or professional theaters either for the stage, the classroom, or as reader's theater.

Copyright law prevents this script from being copied or shared by any technical or digital means.

If you wish to perform this play, you must do the following:

1. Purchase sufficient scripts for your performance :
   - Purchase a Multicopy PDF which allows you to print sufficient copies of this script (one for each cast member, plus 4 for the crew) at Blue Moon Plays. Click Return to Merchant to download your printable PDF. A link to the download will also be emailed to you, along with a link to the application for performance license.

     OR
   - Purchase sufficient printed hard copies (one for each cast member, plus 4 for the crew) - an automatic 10 percent discount is applied to multiple printed hardcopies at the point of ordering.
2. Apply for a performance license.
3. Pay a Performance Fee for the specific days of your performances.

All scripts and licenses shall be obtained at Blue Moon Plays at www.havescripts.com

If you wish to make changes in the script of any kind, you must receive permission from the publisher or the playwright. Permission is usually granted readily when schools or theaters face casting problems and the changes do not affect the quality or intent of the original.

**For information, visit www.havescripts.com;
email info@bluemoonplays.com; or call 757-816-1164**

BROKEN DOLLS

Time: the present
Place: a waiting room at a social service facility.

Set: An empty space with five armless chairs: three in the back row facing front; two in the front facing in profile.

The scenes switch back and forth from the present to flashbacks in the past. Lighting creates the illusion of going into the past.

The characters are all women in their 20's.

Cast:
Blanca: Guatemalan
Adhira: Indian
Sofia: Romanian
Hailey: African American
A-Huei: Taiwanese

SCENE ONE
Lights come up on the waiting room: In the back row, left to right: Hailey; Blanca; an empty chair. In front, left to right: Sofia; Adhira. Hailey has a small end table next to her chair with a few magazines.

Moments of silence. Hailey and Blanca are looking at magazines.

Blanca:
This is my first time here. What about you?

Adhira:
Yes.

Blanca:
How did you find this place?

Adhira:
A woman on the street gave me this address. Told me it's safe.

Blanca nods and returns to reading her magazine. Adhira turns and watches Sofia.

Sofia opens up her bag and takes out a small knife. She looks at it for a moment, then puts it back. She takes a pill bottle out of her bag.

Adhira
What's your name?

Sofia turns away.

Flashback as lights change and Sofia remembers the last time someone asked for her name. Blanca and Hailey stand up and "enter" her memory and whisper.

Blanca & Hailey (overlapping):
What's your name?

Sofia shakes her head.

Hailey:
You don't have to tell, if you don't want to.

Sofia:
I'd rather forget.
I'd rather not be
who I was...

Blanca:
What should we call her?

Hailey:
Something foreign. From Europe…

Sofia.
I like Sofia.

Hailey & Blanca (*overlapping)*
Sofia… Sofia

Sofia:
Sofia?

Blanca:
So pretty.

Sofia looks down at the pill bottle in her hands.

Hailey:
Take one. You'll feel better.

Sofia:
What?

Sophia shakes her head "No".

Hailey:
Take it or you'll hurt my feelings.
Why do you want to hurt my feelings?

Sofia:
I got rid of feeling…

it interfered

with my skin,
who needs extra layers,
I have bones,
a handful of organs,
I don't know how to hurt...

Blanca:
Take it or she'll be mad.

Sofia:
Why are you talking like that,
with your fist like an orange,
your jaw like a brick

Hailey:
Are you trying to make me mad?

Sofia shakes her head "no" and mimes putting a pill in her mouth.

Blanca:
Good. Smart girl. Now some lipstick. Turn your head; close
your eyes.
Purple or pink?

Hailey:
Pink.

Blanca and Hailey disappear.

Sofia:
My eyes run,
silently,
the chemical sting
of powder, of paint,
I've never been painted,
I hate it.

I exhale,
when they pull my hair,
I inhale,

otherwise there's no sound,
but their chatter

Good girl…smart girl…so pretty…

Flashback ends. Lights return to present. Hailey and Blanca
are looking at their magazines as before.

Adhira:
Repeats her question but a bit louder this time.
What's your name?

Sofia takes a pill. Then puts the bottle back in her bag.

SCENE TWO

Blanca:
My name is Blanca.

Adhira:
I'm Adhira. Where do you come from?

Blanca:
I come from a village in Guatemala where the mountains meet
the sea. If I close my eyes, I can see it so clearly, I can almost
touch it. We are farmers. We rent land and grow sugarcane to
sell. Whatever money is leftover, we keep. We use the animals
to help us, if we can. Or we use animals for food. This is our life.

My father hears neighboring villages are sending people north to work on American soil, and he thinks about going. He finds out only young people are allowed. I want to go. He says a girl shouldn't go on a journey like that by herself. But there will be other people my age. Besides, I'm used to working the land. If I could make American money doing the same work I do in the village...It's also a way for me to explore. I've never been further than the nearest village. I didn't know that once you leave, you don't come back.

Adhira:
You don't come back.

Adhira rubs her hands a bit and then takes a lotion bottle out of her bag.

Blanca:
And where do you come from?

Adhira:
India.

A door opens and A-Huei enters. She stops and looks around at the others. Then closes the door and sits down.

The others are watching A-Huei, except for Sofia. Then Hailey & Blanca go back to their magazines.

Adhira has turned toward A-Huei, watching her. Then she turns front. She looks down at her hands, her skin is raw and painful. She massages her hands and remembers a hotel recruit.

Flashback as lights change to past.

A-Huei:
What kind of people do you work for?

Adhira:
'We' work for. There are the ones who brought us here, and there are the managers, who pay them. Both keep track of our pay.

A-Huei:
Where do you live? Here?

Adhira:
No, no. I live in a smaller building called a motel. It's close enough to walk. They keep you there for a month to make sure you're a good worker. After they move you, you're allowed to walk to and from the hotel by yourself.

A-Huei:
When do we get paid?

Adhira:
I'm not sure.

A-Huei:
What do you mean?

Adhira:
I haven't gotten any pay since I started. They keep it because I owe the man that brought me. I hold the door open for guests and welcome them inside, which I and the others like us, scrub clean from six o' clock in the morning until eleven o' clock at night. We are only to rest during our breaks. If we pause during work, a manager comes and yells at us. We have a 30-minute break for lunch in the early afternoon. There are cameras everywhere and there's always someone following our every move.

Hailey Enters memory as hotel manager.

Hailey:

Get to work! We are not paying you to stand around and talk!

Adhira hides the bottle behind her back.

Adhira:
You're not paying us at all. Where are our wages from the last four weeks?

Hailey:
That's fifty dollars I'm deducting from your pay. And you still owe over $5,000. Anything else you want to say?

Hailey disappears.

Adhira:
They deduct if we talk back. They deduct if we stay a minute over our 30-minute lunch break. They deduct if we leave a few minutes early or arrive a few minutes late.

A-Huei:
Do you know how much you owe?

Adhira:
I'm not sure. Somewhere between around $2,000 for special documents; $12,000 for travel expenses; it goes on.

A-Huei:
Don't you want to know?

Adhira:
Why?

A-Huei:
So you can leave?

Adhira:

8

Everybody wants to leave. No one gets to. The hotel has our passports, birth certificates, temporary visas. There's no way out.

Maybe what we owe isn't even real. Maybe the numbers mean nothing, and no one is keeping track of anyone's debt.

A-Huei:
This is a nice hotel – isn't it?

Hailey: *reappears*
Hey. The guest in 305 wants his room cleaned.

Adhira:
At nine o' clock at night?

Hailey:
Which one of you is going?

Adhira:
Don't you think it's strange?

Hailey raises her hand to slap her.

Hailey:
Hey you…do as you're told or I'll….

A-Huei
It's fine. I'll go.

Flashback ends.

Silence.

Hailey is looking through another magazine; Adhira puts lotion bottle back in her bag. She takes out a book she's been reading. Sofia is in her own world – dreaming.

A-Huei takes out a photo from her back and looks at it.
Blanca watches A-Huei.

Blanca:
Do you speak English?

E -A-Huei:
A little.

Blanca:
Where are you from?

A-Huei:
From Taiwan.

Blanca:
Why did you come here?

A-Huei:
I was working in a restaurant; a man said I could make more money as a nanny and gave me an address. They said their nanny had gone so I could do it. I wanted to make more money to give my family, so I went. They had five children. I took care of them. I had to cook, clean, do laundry, yard work, and take care of the children.

A-Huei:
When the regular nanny came back, the family offered to send me out of the country, to work for their friends. They showed me pictures. Big house. Big family. I thought I'd learn English. And make money to send back to my family. So I came here.

Blanca:
What was that like?

A-Huei:

I was working 16 hours a day- cleaning, taking care of the kids. No days off. Had to get up at 4am. The mother didn't want to hear anything about her kids. So they were my kids; not hers.

A-Huei:
I miss my mother. She used to sing to me.
She sings a verse of a song.

The song is giving Sofia a headache. She covers her ears.

SCENE THREE

Hailey:
What exactly is this place?

Blanca:
I think it's a shelter.

Hailey:
A shelter? What do they do here? Who are we waiting for?

Blanca:
I don't know exactly. I guess the person in charge.
It's safe here. They must be busy.

Haley:
How much longer do we have to wait? I don't like being kept waiting.

Lights change to flashback scene.

Hailey:
They know
I've been taking time,
taking time with clients,
making small talk,
taking time from the day,

taking pay from the hands
of the handler,
trying to make any talk,
trying to take the edge off
the daily,
trying to take time off
from the grind,
the clients like how I talk,
like how I dream,
I tell them I've seen boats full of women.

I don't say they're celebrating
the end of men.

Sofia:
You like keeping me waiting, dontcha. I don't like being kept
waiting.

You spent an extra fifteen minutes with number four.

Hailey:
So.

Sofia:
He didn't pay for the extra.

Hailey:
Oh.

Sofia:
Or did he?

Hailey:
No.

Sofia:

You like him?

Sofia:
No.

Sofia:
What about number six?

Hailey:
Don't remember.

Sofia:
An extra ten minutes...

Without extra pay.

Hailey:
Oh.

Sofia:
That's all you have to say? Look at me when I talk to you.

Hailey turns toward her.
Sofia raises her arm and enacts a backward slap.

Sofia:
You made me do that.

Hailey
First time in a long time,
I've been hit.
Across the lip,
starts as a rip,
after another five,
it's a gash,
crawling jagged
from chin to eye.

Thought they'd only try
to make me cry.
Why leave a mark
this dark,

who's gonna pick a girl
with a face tattoo
the shape of a man's hate?

I watch from outside
my body,
the battering,
the wordless lesson,
the other women
looking on, flinching
each time she
makes contact.
Can't hear,
Can't feel,
Can only watch
the fire spread,
the bruises darken,
the gulf widens between me and the girl I see.

Flashback ends and lights return to the present at same time as Hailey's line.

Hailey:
Kept waiting…. kept waiting…

Blanca:
Someone will come.

SCENE FOUR
Hailey takes a bottle wrapped in a paper bag out of her backpack and takes a few drinks out of it during the next

14

scene. A-Huei begins to sing her song again while holding the photo.

Sofia:
Why are you singing? It's giving me a headache.

A-Huei puts the photo back in her bag.

Adhira:
Don't talk to her that way. Leave her alone.

Sofia shrugs.

Blanca:
Why did you come here?

Adhira:
A childhood friend had been working at a hotel. She sent me a letter, "Adhira, you must come and join me…the hotel is so nice." She made it sound like she had it so good in her letter. When I got that letter, I thought 'she sounds so different…so glamorous.' I couldn't pretend I was happy sitting around my parents' house, after my husband went away "on business" and we never heard from him again. There was nothing to do…no jobs for anyone.

When I got there and started the work, I didn't know whether to laugh or scream. I didn't have the courage to hit my friend, but I wanted to. Oh, I wanted to. Why did I ever let myself be fooled by her? How could I be so stupid?? I didn't tell her this: she looked completely different from the person I knew. Thin and sallow. Older. And, her knuckles were raw. "From what?" I wondered.

I held the door open for guests and welcomed them inside, which I and my friend, and others like us, scrubbed clean from six o'clock in the morning to eleven o'clock at night.

Blanca:
How much did you make?

Adhira:
We could keep whatever tips the guests left behind. Ten dollars a week was my average. We were only to rest during our allotted breaks. I learned that if I could clean three rooms at a breakneck pace, I could have a 15-minute nap before I needed to move on to the next three. We had our meals at the hotel--in the beginning they cost nothing; later they began charging us a 'staff rate'. Still, it was cheaper than anywhere else. And we had no place to cook.

Blanca:
Where did the maids come from?

Adhira:
Hard to say, exactly.

Blanca:
Were they legal?

Adhira:
I'm not sure. The managers had different arrangements with the contractors.

Blanca:
You mean traffickers? I read about them – they make billions off our backs.

Hailey takes a drink out of her bottle.

Hailey:
Why can't we order pizza?
I haven't had one

in so long,
I forget,
what it tastes like,
what it looks like,
what it smells like.
I used to like it, is all I remember.

Sofia:
Pizza??? *She laughs.*

Instead of pizza,
something darker,
junk in my veins…
starting days of,
weeks of,
months of,

half-floating,
in the air,
half aware
of what's happening to the body
I used to know.
These are the days,
the weeks,
the months,
of forgetting,
retreat
into dark back alleys
of the mind.

If I'm not in bed,
I'm dreaming
about being there.

Never over. I want to forget…forget…

Hailey:

Never Over.

Hailey takes another drink out of her bottle but it's empty. She turns it upside down.

Sofia:
Never over.

Hailey:
One o' clock
two o' clock
three o' clock
Four o' clock,
five o'clock
six...
arms...voices...a bare floor...
a door opens, closes,
opens, closes,
voices...warm...
hissing...hissing...

Sometimes, different scenarios,

Sofia:
Sometimes, different objects,

Hailey:
Sometimes, different words
for different clients.

Sofia:
6 days a week, 10...20 clients a day...

Blanca:
What's your name?

Hailey:

Hailey.

Blanca:
From where?

Hailey:
Milwaukee; then my pimp moved us around – Detroit; Fargo; Houston…wherever…

What about you? What was the trip like, going "Norte"?

Blanca:.
A truck, then a train, and a bus. Ours was a truck ride from hell. There were two drivers. They feed us twice a day, little patties made of corn. We drink rainwater, collected in containers attached to the back of the truck.

The day we leave the mountains, we also leave the truck. The guide tells everyone that we are, in fact, free to leave whenever we like, however for most of us, the deeds to our homes have been signed over by our parents and can only be returned when we repay the cost of our transport. This is the first I've heard of the deal that's been struck. I ask how much each of us costs to take north. He says each one is $15,000 dollars.

A-Huei:
What kind of work did you do?

Blanca:
The guide took us to an egg farm. When we arrive, a farm manager tells the guide to drive us to a building at the end of the road, where we'll be living. The farm is very big with many buildings. Our building already has people living in it, but there are two empty rooms that are ours. Each room has beds stacked on top of each other, a large bucket, a window, and a light bulb. Outside there is a shower stall next to a toilet. The

chicken house is a large wooden building with rows of wooden shelves where the chickens live and lay their eggs. Our job is to collect their eggs every hour. The chickens scratch at you constantly and you have to be careful or they could scratch you in the eye. We work 14 hours every day.

It's not the way I imagined farm work would be. If we don't finish the work we're given, it's held against our debt. Maria, who's been here six months, says that the debt takes fifteen years to repay. Weekends there is only work, though we have the option of not working on Sunday, but most of us choose to work because it gets us closer to paying our debts.

A-Huei:
Did you make any money?
Blanca:
Not a cent.

Hailey:
The pimp promised lots of money to work in a massage parlor. It turned out to be a brothel, where they lined us up. A man came, chose two of us, paid the pimp. They shook hands. The man took us to his hotel – for a week. Another man took us for almost a month.

The men were all ages...rich...poor...Americans...foreigners...all types. We were girls, boys, trans...some only 10 years old. If we tried to run, the pimp beat us – with his hands, with his feet. He beat me on the street. Everyone going by could see. I thought someone would stop and say something. I felt like I wasn't
even there. I was numb.
Promises...promises...

Sofia hums the melody from a song she remembers and sways as she sings.

20

Sofia:
He promised me...a career...dancing...

He told my mother – "look...instead of being poor, instead of begging...let her come with me outside the country. She'll have money and she'll send you money."

Adhira:
Where were you?

Sofia:
In Romania. He said he'd meet me at the airport. When I got there, the airline agent said she had no record of my name in their system. Then he arrived and told the agent that he had my boarding pass. He said the travel agency asked him to hold onto it for safekeeping.

It turned out the name on the boarding pass was...not mine. It matched the name on the passport that I was given, which I'd exchanged for my actual passport. He said I'd get my passport back upon arrival. He said he was hired by my employer to escort me and two others. The 'others' were girls, four or five years younger. They didn't talk much; instead they held hands and didn't seem to want to let go. Throughout the long flight, I dreamed of my new life.

When we landed, he started yelling: "We're late. Get your things. Follow me." It was dark when we stopped at a two-story building. It looked abandoned. We entered a smelly room behind the stairs. He told us this would be where we would sleep. Except there were three of us, and only one bed. One small bed, that looked like it belonged to a child. Before anyone could say anything, the door closed. And locked. 'Who do you think you are?' I went to the door. 'Open this door! Open it!!' I banged on it. I tried to open the window, but it wouldn't move. I looked out, and saw the car driving away! 'What is going on?

What are we doing here??' I turned around. The girls were in the corner, holding hands, shaking.

In the morning, he began shouting at us: "Up! Get up!" It was still dark out. With a flashlight in our faces, we were being rushed out of the room. I hated that room, so good riddance. But where were we going? One of the girls started crying. He yelled for us to get in the car. I got in the car. Looked back. I immediately regretted looking. I turned away. I heard something hard strike against flesh. I didn't want to know. We got in the car. We were being driven away.

Adhira:
Where did he take you?

Sofia:
To dance...at a club.

A-Huei:
Show us.

Sofia rises and begins her dance, humming to the music she remembers.

Sofia:
Start slow,
speed up,
hold back,
release.
Pulls one of her straps off her shoulder.

Start slow,
speed up,
hold back,
release.

Pulls the other strap off her shoulder and continues to dance.

Adhira rises and does an Indian folk dance.

A-Huei rises, performing her native dance and singing along with it.

Blanca and Hailey watch them dance.

During the dance, Sofia turns, her back in frame, and lifts her hair above her head. There's a tattoo on her upper back in large letters: "PROPERTY OF…ZD"
Then she turns front, still holding her hair up.

Blanca:
Property of…ZD??? What does that mean – property of…

Sofia stops dancing, returns to her chair and sits down, her back to the others.

Adhira, and A-Huei stop dancing and sit down.

Silence.

SCENE FIVE

A-Huei takes a stuffed toy dog out of her bag and plays with it.

Hailey tries to regain the good mood they were all in. She remembers a Motown song she used to like and starts singing a bit of it. Then she stops.

A-Huei:
That's pretty. Sing more.

Hailey:

The first boy I ever kissed - I was fifteen; he was seventeen. We sang that song together at my cousin's birthday party. I had no idea who he was. We finished, and I turned to him. And we kissed!

I was so shy. But I had a feeling that if I didn't do it the moment would be gone. We had such a strong connection when we were singing.

Adhira:
You married him?

Hailey:
It turned out he wanted a physical connection, no other kind.

Blanca:
Surprise.

Hailey
I was such a fool. Everything he did, everything he said, I saw through love-struck glasses. When I got pregnant, he wanted me to get rid of the baby, I said, 'let's get married!' I wanted a wedding at sunset. He wanted to find himself. He said he was leaving.

Blanca:
And that was that.

Hailey:
Well...no... I followed him. He wasn't happy to see me. He hurt me. Told me to leave him alone. I had the baby. And I gave him away. My parents didn't want to deal with me. I ran away. And that was that.

Blanca:
Boys...we were all about the same age on the truck: fourteen, fifteen. Most are boys but there is another girl. Naturally, we become friends. I'm stronger than she is, and I protect her from

two of the boys – they keep teasing her as we ride through the mountains, calling her 'skinny' and making faces, and she cries. I go up to them and hit them both in the face, with my hand, like this, in a ball. After that, they stop.

Sofia:
I think: I know boys,
I think: I know boys trying to be men,
I think I know,
though these boys are not
the ones I was raised on.
They are no one's,
hazy-eyed and sharp-toothed,
belonging nowhere.
Mine at least knew,
when to stop playing rough.
These couldn't be rough enough.
They threw me,
back and forth,
room to room,
I exploded inside,
again and again,

They laughed,

I learned...you are not enough.

Adhira:
You are not enough.
for help,
for care,
for saving,
from being burned.

Silence.

Flashback as Blanca and A-Huei rise and "enter" Adhira's memory; the lights change. Blanca points at A-Huei's arm.

Blanca:
What's that?

A-Huei:
A-Huei covers her arm.
Don't know.

Blanca:
No bruises. We should never be able to see bruises.
It ruins the experience.

Adhira:
Who knows better than you?

Blanca:
What?
Did you hear how she spoke to me?

A-Huei:
I did.

Blanca::
Was that a compliment or an insult?

Adhira:
Pick the one you like.

Blanca:
If you don't like it here, you can leave! Oh...and don't forget your passport.

Blanca laughs and disappears.

26

Adhira:
What about the room you cleaned last week?

A-Huei:
What about it.

Adhira:
You and I know that no room ever needs cleaning at night.

You're so skinny...is that a cut?
You have to hide it.

You got hurt again. They were talking about firing you. Nobody
wants a sick girl. I told them you were strong and a hard
worker. I convinced them to keep you.

A-Huei:
I know.

Adhira:
Now get to work...they are watching you closely now.
There's nothing we can do...no papers...

Flashback ends as lights return to present.

Adhira:
You are not enough...not enough.

A-Huei is still playing with the toy dog.

Adhira:
I think about whether I should have stayed and whether going
to a new place with new people is a good idea.

Are you a slave if you never want to leave?

Sofia:
Sold...a slave...

A-Huei:
My room was a large closet with a mattress on the floor. I ate
what they left on their plates. I waited on everyone...The
mother was always complaining. 'You call this clean?' Then she
beat me. But I loved the children and they loved me. So I
stayed.

Blanca:
How much did you make?

A-Huei:
They were rich. They told me it would be less than they
promised because my plane ticket was very expensive. They
promised me an allowance. I never got it.

Sofia:
Sold...a slave...for sex...

A-Huei:
Sold for sex??

Sofia:
I want to run away...run...away...

Flashback as lights change.

Hailey:
Don't run away.
Runaways turn up in the park.

Nobody cares about you
if they find you in the park.

Sofia:

28

Nobody cares anyway.

Hailey:
Oh, no. Not true.
I do.

I have a feeling every one of your clients will, too.

Sofia:
Okay.

Hailey:
Why aren't you excited?
Are you excited on the inside?
You don't have to be emotional. It's more interesting if you're not.
This way, nothing is off-limits to the clients.

They really like you.
They would have left us...
They keep us alive.

Don't interfere with that.
And we won't interfere with you.

Flashback ends as lights return to the present.
SCENE SIX

Sofia:
Though I was older,
going on sixteen,

I was their golden goose
and they all knew it,
hated it,
loved it,
hated me,

worshipped me,
such a thing,
such a human
thing,
to be opposite ends
of being,
at the same time,
in the same person.

Hailey:
Hard pulls,
shocks to scalp,
fingers scraping
through hair
that once belonged to me,
now his,
without shame,
I'm spoiled
I'm spoiled
Or saved...
which one
which one am I...

Hailey:
One of the girls was only 13, forced to have sex with one man
after another. Sometimes 30 – 40 men a day. She was
ashamed...as if she had done something wrong. She tried to
escape.

The pimp beat her in front of us to set an example. Then he
choked her...burned her...she never tried to run again.

As she remembers hearing the pimp's threat - in a man's voice:
I'll kill you if you try to run.

Sofia:

She rises...her hand brandishing a small knife - in a man's voice.
Next time, I'll kill you.

At the sight of the knife, Blanca, Adhira, and A-Huei rise from their seats.

Hailey:
We beat them. Sometimes we rape them.

Sofia:
We call it 'washing the hands". *Hailey & Sofia laugh.*

Hailey:
You're sold...a slave.

Blanca:
I am not your slave.

Adhira:
We are not slaves.

Hailey:
You still owe me $10,000.

Sofia: *lowers the knife.*
I have your papers. Where will you go?

A-Huei:
I go back home...to my family.

Adhira:
I'm leaving. It's my life.

Sofia:
raising the knife again.

You are not enough.

Adhira:
I am enough.

Sofia:
I'll kill you if you run.

Hailey:
You will have nightmares about me for the rest of your life.

You are mine...my property!

Sofia: *slowly lowering the knife as she comes out of the play-acting.*
Property...I am not your property. My name is Nadia... *She sits down.*
My name is Nadia...

Blanca, A-Huei, and Adhira sit back down.

A few moments of silence.

Blanca:
Never over...never over...

I never thought I'd be owned by another human being until it happened.

A-Huei:
I was owned...wasn't allowed out of the house. Couldn't even use the phone...not allowed to call my family. I asked if I could make one phone call. She refused..said I was worthless. I yelled back at her. She slapped me and told me to get out. I was out on the street.

Adhira:

Seven days,
15 hours a day,
four weeks,
twelve months.

No emotion
became the standard.
I was told to teach it
to recruits

Tough...Tough
was our motto.
Tough luck...tough skin...
Became tough competition
For scraps.

Blanca:
They're supposed to be people
People who look out for you.

Hailey:
No one looks out for you...
You look out for you...
Look out for yourself...

A - Huei:
Where do you go
if you don't know
anyone, anywhere?

Sofia:
I go back,
to a rough house,
not the same one,
this one lasted,
was full,
wall to wall,

with temporary bodies,
permanently scarred.
They circled like sharks.

Rescue…waiting for rescue.
She laughs.

Blanca:
I start having dreams about escaping. I've never had them
before. The dreams are sweet. I hear my mother's voice: stand
up straight.
Keep looking ahead; keep making me proud.

A-Huei:
How did you escape?

Blanca:
We were told not to trust the police. That they arrest people
like us because we have no papers.

But a few years after, the police come. I hear the manager
yelling. They're here because of us. All the workers are taken
away from the farm. The owner and managers are taken away
too. I get on a big bus full of people. At the police station, they
give me this address…say here they'll help me…so I come.

Adhira:
I trained the new maids. One of them was ordered to clean a
room at night. An hour later she came back, with bruises on her
wrists, a cut on her mouth.

One night, one of my maids walked into a room. A man was
waiting for her. She walked over to the open window and
jumped. I packed my bag and walked out.

Sofia rises and moves forward.

Sofia:
So slowly,
did I,
get up,
and walk out that door,
whether from exhaustion…

junk in my veins…
I know I walked out,

On that room…

Hailey rises and moves toward Sofia.

Hailey:
on the men who should have helped
and should have listened,
who told me I had better shut up
or I'd be arrested too.

A-Huei rises and moves forward.

A-Huei:
I walked out to the street…
I looked left,
looked right,
nowhere to go…

Adhira:
I walked out to the street…
I looked up…

and went in the direction of the sun.

The women look up at the imagined sky.

They freeze.

Lights dim.   Same house music as at the beginning of play fades in.

Curtain.

www.ingramcontent.com/pod-product-compliance
Lightning Source LLC
LaVergne TN
LVHW021549080426
835509LV00019B/2917